Late, but great

Looking cute as a bundle Princess Charlotte Elizabeth Diana may have arrived a few days after her due date, but no-one was complaining when she was revealed to the world for the first time

CONTENTS

A Mirror publication

Head of Syndication & Licensing: Fergus McKenna

Mirrorpix: David Scripps, Simon Flavin

020 7293 3858

Produced by Trinity Mirror Media

PO BOX 48, Liverpool L69 3EB

ISBN 9781910335192

Managing Director: Steve Hanrahan

Commercial Director: Will Beedles

Executive Editor: Paul Dove

Executive Art Editor: Rick Cooke

Produced by: Roy Gilfoyle

Designed by: Colin Sumpter

Written by: Chris Brereton, Chris McLoughlin

Part of the Mirror Collection

© Published by Trinity Mirror 2015

Images: Mirrorpix, PA Photos

Printed by William Gibbons

Welcome
TO THE
Family

She arrived fashionably late, but
Princess Charlotte was worth
the wait as the perfect family
just got even more perfect

'It means a great deal to the Duke and Duchess that so many people have celebrated the arrival of their new daughter'

She took her time in coming, but when she arrived she was a sight to behold.

The arrival of Princess Charlotte Elizabeth Diana Cambridge may have been delayed by 10 days but the world still came to a standstill to welcome the royal family's newest addition.

In the build-up to the birth, the Duchess of Cambridge did everything she could to maintain her normal schedule including exercising as usual – and running round after Prince George, the 21-month-old who also dominated the headlines when he was born in July 2013.

In fact, the Duchess of Cambridge was so late, the parking restrictions outside the Lindo Wing of St Mary's Hospital in Paddington had to be extended by another week.

However, the waiting and the wondering finally stopped

on Saturday, May 2 when royal family fans and the media camped outside the hospital were told that the Duchess of Cambridge had arrived from Kensington Palace and was inside giving birth.

And at 8.34am, just two hours later, the royal family had its newest member, weighing a very happy and healthy 8lbs 3oz.

The good news was first announced on Kensington Palace's Twitter account at 11.09am before the tradition and pageantry that ensures the royal family remain a worldwide fascination kicked into top gear.

At 12.30, a gold easel appeared from the Privy Purse Door at Buckingham Palace and was placed on the forecourt.

Attached to it was a note signed and framed by medics from the Lindo Wing and it read: "Her Royal Highness, the

LINDO WING

A delighted Duchess waves to the public, clutching her new baby daughter, with her husband at her side

Grandparents arrive

Left:
Prince Charles, his wife Camilla and Carole Middleton – joined by daughter Pippa – are pictured arriving at Kensington Palace

Right:
Kate gazes adoringly at the little girl she gave birth to only hours earlier

Duchess of Cambridge was safely delivered of a daughter at 8.34 today."

Hundreds queued up in the bad weather to read the easel while a town crier, Tony Appleton, also rang his bell outside the hospital and announced the news to the world.

The reaction from around the planet was immediate and magnificent as Tower Bridge looked aglow as it was bathed in pink light while the BT Tower flashed pink with the words 'IT'S A GIRL' adorned on it to let London's workers and tourists know the news.

In a message for Prince George, sailors aboard HMS Lancaster even lined up to spell out the word 'SISTER' on their deck.

A Royal spokesman added: "The Duke and Duchess are hugely grateful for the messages of congratulations they have received from all over the world.

"It means a great deal to them that so many people have celebrated the arrival of their new daughter."

The birth of Princess Charlotte appears to have been relatively straightforward – and certainly speedy – and the Duchess of Cambridge was in fine spirits almost straightaway.

Unlike Prince George's arrival, which saw her stay in overnight, mother and daughter were fit and healthy enough to leave just 10 hours after the delivery.

There was just time for Prince William to pop home and bring George to the hospital to meet his new sister before she was shown to the public for the first time on the steps of the Lindo Wing.

The Duchess of Cambridge looked stunning as she left the hospital in a yellow dress while proud dad Prince William walked by her side, grinning wildly at his new daughter before he drove the pair back to Kensington Palace.

The Duchess' recovery was stunning and it was a good job too as she had visitors queuing up to see her newborn daughter back at Kensington Palace the following day.

The day after giving birth, both sets of grandparents popped round for a cuppa and a cuddle as the Duchess of Cambridge's mum Carole, dad Michael and her sister Pippa drove through the gates at 11.30am before Prince Charles and Camilla followed soon after.

The beaming smile on Prince Charles' face perfectly captured how delighted he was to get a granddaughter after previously expressing his desire for Prince George to have a baby sister.

From Australia, Prince Charlotte's uncle, Prince Harry, also joined in the celebrations and expressed his delight. He is on a tour of Australia as part of his army duties but tweeted his happiness.

Meet your sister

Left:
William brings Prince George to the hospital to meet his new sister

Left, inset:
William is pictured after visiting new brother Harry in hospital in 1984

William completes his fatherly duties and signals to the media how many children he now has!

He wrote: "She is absolutely beautiful. I can't wait to meet her."

Next up to see the latest addition to her family was the Queen and Prince Philip who were in Sandringham when little Princess Charlotte was born but caught up with her when they returned.

The birth of Princess Charlotte is expected to lead to a huge economic boost for Britain with a projected £80m worth of goods on sale to celebrate her arrival.

Mugs, baby dresses, plates and T-shirts are all flying off the shelves and the phrase 'royal baby' was the most searched-for term on Google in the 24 hours after her birth.

Princess Charlotte, of course, has no idea yet that her arrival caused glee and celebrations across the globe and she has many happy years as a lucky little girl ahead of her before any real royal duties will come her way.

Those years will be spent at Anmer Hall on the Sandringham estate where Princess Charlotte will run and play with her brother Prince George and her besotted parents.

It will be an idyllic childhood followed by a wonderful life but, in many ways, she is no different to any other baby.

She is adored, cherished and loved by her close family and brings delight to all who meet her.

She is very much a product of the modern royal family where love comes above everything else.

It will be exciting to watch her grow up alongside her brother and parents.

And, who knows, maybe Princess Charlotte herself will one day be able to celebrate a younger brother or sister of her own...

A nation celebrates

It's up there in lights as Tower Bridge, the BT Tower and the London Eye are lit up in celebration while royal fans marked the occasion in their own special way

Bottom right:
The traditional easel at Buckingham Palace brings news of the birth

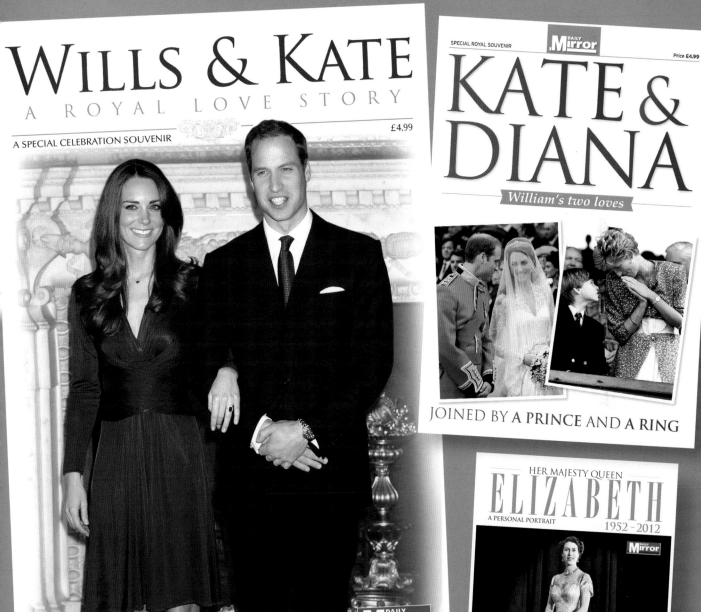

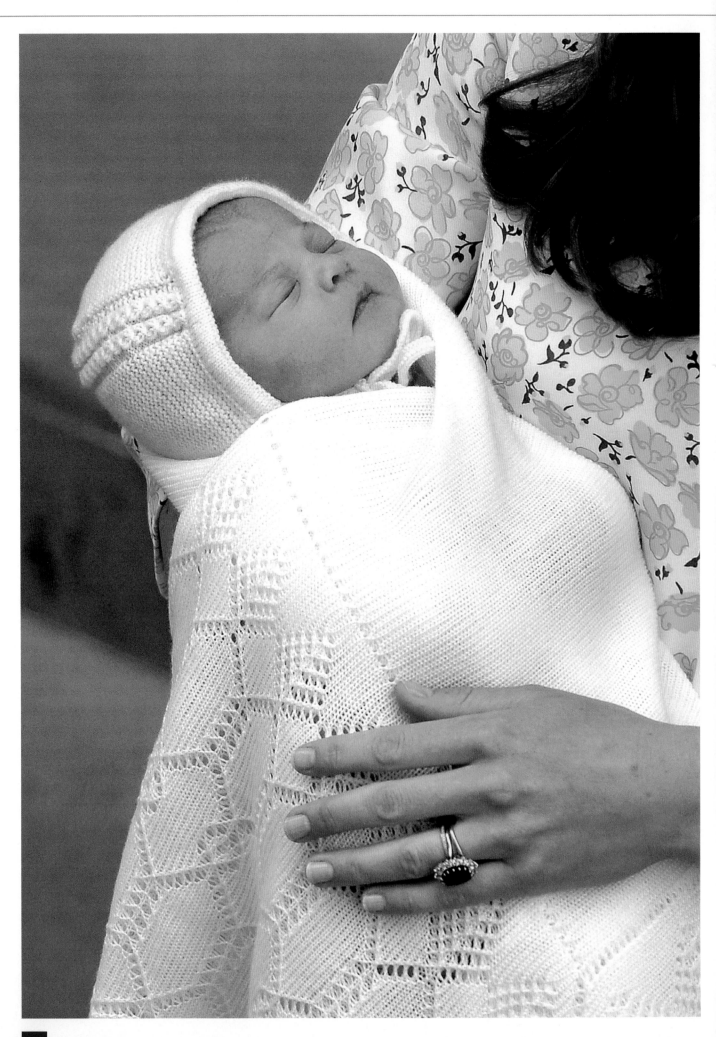

Charlotte
ELIZABETH DIANA

A beautiful baby deserves a beautiful name...and that is what she got

Her Royal Highness Princess Charlotte of Cambridge, to give the newest member of the royal family her formal name.

Or maybe, to her inner circle – those closest to her – she'll be Charley. Or Lottie. Her mum and dad, after all, are affectionately known as Kate and Wills by so many.

Catherine and William. The Duke and Duchess of Cambridge. It somehow feels a little too formal to a younger generation of Brits who, perhaps more than ever before, feel a sense of identification with the second in line to the throne, his elegant wife and their gorgeous young family. Charlotte will be loved a lot.

But why Charlotte?

It's not a name recently associated with the royals. It's a bit different. Distinctive. Although in the coming months there will presumably be an influx of babies named Charlotte across our green and pleasant land in the same way that school classrooms will, in a couple of years, see an increased number of boys called George in honour of the new princess's big brother.

The Duke and Duchess of Cambridge effectively honoured both royal tradition and the most loved women in their lives by naming their baby daughter Charlotte Elizabeth Diana.

Paying tribute to the much-missed Diana, Princess of Wales, and the Queen, those middle name choices were not especially surprising – and the bookies will also tell you the princess's first name was, along with Alice, a heavily backed selection – but in opting for Charlotte they've found a name that also resonates with the Middleton family,

Meaning 'petite', Charlotte is, in French, the feminine form of Charles, a fitting tribute to the Prince of Wales, who made no secret of his desire for a granddaughter.

Charlotte also happens to be the middle name of the Duchess's sister, Pippa Middleton, and goes back in her family to her paternal great-great-great-grandmother Charlotte Ablett, born in 1825.

It is also a name with royal pedigree. Queen Charlotte and Princess Charlottes have existed before.

Although born Sophie in 1744, Queen Charlotte, who was married to George III, shunned her Christian name to go by the title.

She was Queen of Great Britain and Ireland from their marriage in 1761 until the union of the two kingdoms in 1801, after which she was Queen of the United Kingdom of Great Britain and Ireland until her death in 1818.

Queen Charlotte bore King George III 15 children and helped found Kew Gardens. It's also worth noting that Queen Charlotte's & Chelsea Hospital, which is named after her, is part of the same NHS Trust as St Mary's Hospital Paddington, where Princess Charlotte was born in the private Lindo Wing.

In 1766, Queen Charlotte gave birth to a daughter, who she called Charlotte. She was known as the Princess Royal.

Her granddaughter – the daughter of George IV and Caroline of Brunswick – was Princess Charlotte of Wales. Born in 1796, had she outlived both her grandfather King George III and her father, she would have become Queen. ➤

Princess of Monaco's daughter, Charlotte Marie Pomeline Casiraghi, pictured in 1997

The picture of happiness, William and Kate show their baby to the media and well-wishers

However, she died aged just 21 in 1817 following childbirth, leading to a mass outpouring of national grief. She was King George IV's only child.

Princess Charlotte also shares a name with a modern-day European princess, but as fourth in line to the throne her chances of becoming monarch are much better.

Charlotte Marie Pomeline Casiraghi, 29, is the second child of Caroline, Princess of Hanover, Princess of Monaco, and the late Stefano Casiraghi, an Italian industrialist. She is eighth in line to the throne of Monaco, but is guaranteed to get rather good seats for the Grand Prix!

It is the choice of Diana, however, as one of the princess's middle names that is clearly the most personal to her father.

The death of Diana, Princess of Wales, in August 1997, when William was just 15, meant the Duke's closest female blood relatives were the Princess Royal and the Queen. It resulted in him longing for a daughter throughout his adult life.

The Duke's mother was the first and only British Princess Diana, and there are no known Dianas in the Duchess's family. Deriving from the Latin Diviana or Divus, it means 'Divine'.

In choosing Elizabeth as a middle name, Charlotte's parents have paid tribute to the Queen in the year she will become Britain's longest-reigning monarch. Elizabeth was also the name of Queen Elizabeth the Queen Mother, who was close to Prince William before her death in 2002.

There are also strong connections to the Middleton family. Both the Duchess of Cambridge and her mother Carole have the middle name of Elizabeth which was passed down from Carole Middleton's grandmother, Elizabeth Temple. Elizabeth means 'oath of God'.

But it is the name Charlotte – the 21st most popular for girls in 2013 according to the Office for National Statistics – that will remain the most talked about as it slips into the consciousness of a nation that has now seen a new prince and princess born in the space of less than two years.

And, amidst all the talk of tradition and historical referencing of why Her Royal Highness Princess Charlotte of Cambridge was so named, one key factor should not be overlooked.

Charlotte is called Charlotte because her mum and dad liked it. Which, as any parent will tell you, is the best baby-naming reason of all.

A 41-gun royal salute in Hyde Park on the day Princess Charlotte was named

Snuggled up tight, the new princess was shown to the world and then named two days later

The LONG WAIT

Preparations for a new arrival can drag on but there's little chance to relax when you're an integral part of the royal family. William and Kate have balanced their duties as parents to George with their many public engagements – as well as making sure they're ready for the addition of a new family member. Here's a look at the busy lives of the Duke and Duchess of Cambridge in the past few months, in particular how Kate bloomed through her long pregnancy...

The Duchess of Cambridge meets Harry Styles from One Direction at the Royal Variety Performance

DAILY **Mirror**
Cowell: It's Round One to Strictly
Why the battle over Scotland matters to YOU

DUCHESS PREGNANT AGAIN

KATE'S SO SICK.. I NEED TO BE WITH HER NOW
Wils' worry as wife too ill for engagements

SEPTEMBER

It was an exciting month in September as the Duke and Duchess of Cambridge announced they were expecting their second child. Kate missed a number of royal engagements after she was struck down with a severe bout of morning sickness, which she also suffered when pregnant with Prince George. As the news travelled, Prince Charles hinted he hoped for a little girl, while Prince Harry joked he wanted to see his brother "suffer more."

And it was a busy month for Prince Harry who hosted his very own Invictus Games — a paralympic-style event for injured service personnel.

Meanwhile, the spotlight was on the Queen, who made a rare comment on politics. Her Majesty urged people to "think very carefully about the future" before the Scottish Independence referendum so she would have been pleased that the Scottish people voted to remain part of the union.

OCTOBER

It was a better month for the Duchess, as she made her first public appearance since suffering from severe morning sickness. Kate looked slightly under the weather when she met the President of Singapore Tony Tan Keng Yam and his wife Mary. The Queen and Prince Phillip also welcomed the president and his wife to Buckingham Palace.

In a month when the Queen sent her first tweet ("It is a pleasure to open the Information Age exhibition today at the @ScienceMuseum and I hope people will enjoy visiting.

Elizabeth R.") the Duchess of Cambridge went to the 2014 Wildlife Photography of the Year awards, which was held at the Natural History Museum, of which Kate is a patron.

NOVEMBER

The Queen and Prince Phillip celebrated their 67th wedding anniversary during a ceremonial RAF fly-past. On a visit to the UK's most northerly RAF base in Moray, the Queen and Duke watched as two Typhoons and a Tornado jet flew over RAF Lossiemouth.

And united in remembrance, the Queen defied terror threats as she led millions of Britons in remembering the fallen. The Queen was pictured laying a wreath at the Cenotaph in Whitehall following the two-minute silence.

Elsewhere, the Duke and Duchess of Cambridge hosted the Royal Variety Performance in the absence of the Queen. Traditionally the Queen has taken it in turns with Prince Charles to attend the evening celebrations, but Kate and William's presence was a sign the younger royals are stepping in to help. Highlights of the evening included the moment Kate and William met One Direction. The royal couple have previously admitted to being huge fans of X-Factor.

The Duchess of Cambridge invited the children's mental health charity Place2Be into her home as she hosted the first ever Place2Be Wellbeing in Schools Awards ceremony. The charity is the leading UK provider of school-based mental health support and counts Kate as one of their patrons.

The expectant couple arrive at the Royal Variety Performance where William met musician Ed Sheeran

William keeps an eye on Kate as they met the President of Singapore and his wife

William joined the Queen at the Cenotaph for Remembrance Sunday in November and his wife at the Tower of London

William and Kate at the
Metropolitan Museum of Art
in New York in December

Above:
A trip across the Atlantic saw the royal couple meet up with President Obama, rapper Jay Z and politician Hillary Clinton

Left:
Kate stops to chat with some children in Harlem

Below:
The Duchess of Cambridge's first engagement of 2015 was to open a new room at Barlby Primary School

DECEMBER

In the final month of the year, it was time for the United States to get a dose of British charm. Kate and William took the US by storm during their three-day groundbreaking tour of the Big Apple.

The couple met up with Hip Hop rapper Jay Z and his pop star wife Beyonce during a basketball game. While, Basketball 'King' Le Bron James broke royal protocol when he put a friendly arm around Kate.

Meanwhile, William spoke of his excitement over the birth of his second child when he met President Barack Obama in the White House.

The royal couple concluded their first taste of the Big Apple by attending a glamorous dinner at the Metropolitan Museum of Art, a fundraiser for their alma mater, St Andrews University, to mark its 600th anniversary. And Kate sprang a major surprise by reaching into her wardrobe and pulling out something she had worn twice before on official engagements – a stunning £3,145 petrol blue Jenny Packham gown.

Just days later the world was treated to a trio of official Christmas photographs of gorgeous George. He's used to being snapped with his parents, but the adorable toddler looked every inch the centre of attention as he beamed in a courtyard at Kensington Palace.

To get in to the Christmas spirit The Duke and Duchess of Cambridge took young George to a Christmas show in the village of Thursford near their home of Anmer Hall. Families were shocked to see the 16-month-old royal toddler touring the Santa's Magical Journey attraction with his parents. The young prince gazed in awe at animated reindeer, penguins, polar bears and elves during his hour-long visit.

JANUARY

A new Twitter account was set up for Prince William, the Duchess of Cambridge and Prince Harry. The aim of the account, which uses the handle @KensingtonRoyal, is to provide the latest updates on the trio and their Royal Foundation charities. They also opened an account on Instagram.

"Hello from Kensington Palace! Welcome to our new Twitter account," said the royals' first tweet.

The Duchess of Cambridge undertook her first engagement of the year at Barlby Primary School. Kate previously had to postpone her engagement there, but this time she was able to attend and show off her prominent baby bump at the north west London school.

As part of her work as Patron of charity The Art Room, Kate officially named The Clore Art Room at the school, before celebrating the dedicated work of foster carers at an event hosted by The Fostering Network.

January also saw the Duchess join families and volunteers at a coffee morning set up by Family Friends, an organisation that provides befriending and mentoring services to families in deprived areas of the borough.

Following her visit to the coffee morning, the pregnant royal formally opened Kensington Aldridge Academy, a new school for pupils aged 11 to 18. She met governors, staff and students before touring the new building and watching part of a lesson. The Duchess also watched a dance performance in the school's theatre and unveiled a plaque before visiting the school's Creates Hub for young entrepreneurs.

Kate also formally opened Kensington Leisure Centre, a new development which replaces the former building where her husband Prince William and brother-in-law Prince Harry had swimming lessons at school.

Blooming marvellous

Keeping an eye on that royal bump as Kate has continued to grow on us

How Kate's tummy grew when she was pregnant with George in 2013...

January 11

February 19

March 5

March 17

March 19

March 20

April 4

April 21

Kate meets Lord Julian Fellowes on the set of Downton Abbey

FEBRUARY

Prince William, the Duchess of Cambridge and their son Prince George returned to British soil after their family holiday in the Caribbean island of Mustique, where they celebrated the 60th birthday of Kate's mum Carole Middleton.

The family were seen boarding a British Airways plane as they prepared to set off from St Lucia's airport following their annual holiday.

After returning from Mustique the Duchess of Cambridge joined Sir Ben Ainslie in Portsmouth to visit the site of Ben Ainslie Racing and the 1851 Trust headquarters.

Kate and her expanding bump also travelled to Staffordshire and the West Midlands to carry out a double engagement in February. Ever the gracious royal, Kate let her maternal side shine through as she made the visit in honour of two charities – the East Anglia's Children's Hospices (EACH) and Action for Children.

The Duchess was touring the Emma Bridgewater factory, where she was able to see how the earthenware products are made and decorated.

She had a go at painting some of the pottery herself, carefully printing colourful butterflies on each mug, as well as taking part in a ceramic painting workship with young children and their parents.

Prince William, meanwhile, announced that he would start flying as an air ambulance pilot in the summer. It had already been announced that William would join the service, based at Cambridge Airport, in spring – but now it's been revealed he won't actually be operational until a few months later.

The pilot-Prince will welcome a few months breathing space as he juggles his new job with a second baby.

MARCH

From one aristocratic George to another, the Duchess of Cambridge received a toy train for her son from the young actor who plays Master George Crawley in Downton Abbey. During her visit to the set of the period drama at Ealing Studios, Kate was given a present for little Prince George of Cambridge by Zac Barker, who stars as Lady Mary's son George alongside his twin brother Oliver in the show.

Britain's royals were out in force at St Paul's Cathedral, with the Duchess of Cambridge joining the Queen, Prince William and Prince Harry at a service marking the end of combat operations in Afghanistan.

The Duke and Duchess were paying a visit to the Mons Barracks – home to 1st Battalion Irish Guards – to view the annual St Patrick's Day parade.

William was attending in his capacity as royal colonel of the regiment, while Kate was accompanying her husband for the same engagement they have fulfilled for the past three consecutive years.

Kate visited a children's centre in Woolwich that is run by charity Home-Start. Kate had the chance to speak to fellow mums and families who use the charity's services, and volunteers who work for the organisation and mentioned that her second baby would be born in 'mid-to-late April'.

During the visit the Duchess, 33, learnt about how the charity helps struggling families and youngsters who are facing all sorts of issues, from isolation, mental ill health, bereavement, multiple births, illness or disability.

From mid-March onwards Kate then began to take a back seat in terms of public engagements as she prepared for life as a mum-of-two.

Above:
Kate helps a pupil at a school in Kent with a collage and receives a sailing shirt from Sir Ben Ainslie in Portsmouth while William sups a pint of Guinness on St Patrick's Day

Left and below:
William feeds an elephant during a trip to China and puts the finishing touches to a statue of Shaun the Sheep on the same excursion

Welcome
TO OUR
WORLD

This is how the early days went for me....
...From your big brother, George

When I was born...

Delighted parents show their son to the world

The enormous press packs sweltered in the heat. Reporters tried their best to fill hours and hours or airtime.

Gossip flew through the air and rumours were rife about if, when and how the Princess of Cambridge – my mum – had given birth.

But, finally, at 8.29pm on July 22, a spokesperson for Clarence House announced in a press release that I had been safely born.

All of a sudden, those same reporters and TV crews had cast-iron happy news to deliver to a world that was hanging off every word.

I had arrived.

However, the action had really begun 14 hours earlier – when I first made clear that the time was here for me to be born.

At 6am, my mum and dad arrived at St Mary's Hospital, Paddington, London, using a back entrance to the Lindo Wing so they could avoid the hundreds of media people present.

Almost two hours later, Kensington Palace finally confirmed that my mummy had gone into labour and that everything was going nicely to plan.

Twitter, Facebook and news channels around the world went into meltdown, especially in the heat, as celebrities ranging from Piers Morgan to John Prescott passed on their good luck messages.

Prime Minister David Cameron then joined in before my grandad, Prince Charles, visiting the National Railway Museum in York, let slip to a member of the public that he had no idea what was happening. "I know absolutely nothing at the moment," he told a member of the public, "we're just waiting to find out."

As lunchtime arrived, thousands of well-wishers started to gather at Buckingham Palace as it became clear that today was the day.

It was a long afternoon as the public and press waited for something to be announced but behind the closed doors of the Lindo Wing, my mum was doing all the hard work, until, at 4.24pm, I was born.

Rumours continued to circulate around the world until that Clarence House press release gave the public the green light to start celebrating.

The announcement of my arrival via a press release was a very modern and savvy way of delivering the news to the world.

However, the royal family I am now a member of are also sticklers for history and tradition and they were not going to miss this opportunity.

As a result, at 8.48pm, a traditional easel, on which royal births had always previously been announced, was placed in the grounds of Buckingham Palace by Badar Azim, a footman with the Royal Household, and Ailsa Anderson, the Queen's press secretary, for the public to read.

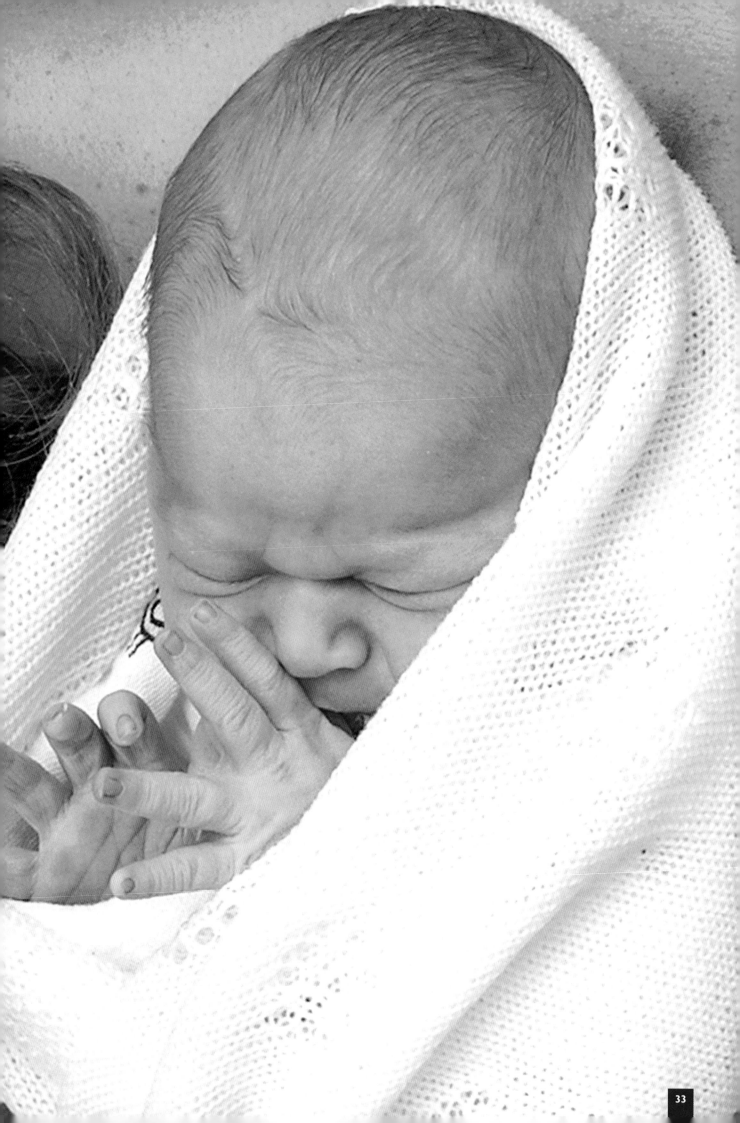

The press pack set up outside St Mary's Hospital

Kate gazes adoringly at her new baby

Royal wave? I've cracked it, mum

£50M ..and you can have Suarez

NEW PRINCE NAMED
BOY GEORGE

(That's His Royal Highness Prince George Alexander Louis of Cambridge.. to be precise)

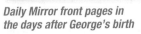

Daily Mirror front pages in the days after George's birth

The epitome of proud parents with their bundle of joy

*Above and left:
William carefully carries his new
son while the gathered crowds
and media get their first glimpse
of the royal arrival*

*Below: Westminster City Council
registrar Alison Cathcart holds
a copy of the birth register for
Prince George*

As night falls people are still gathered at Buckingham Palace where an easel was placed to announce the arrival of a new royal baby on July 22, 2013

With a new family member on board Prince William prepares to drive home

A family photo taken at the home of Kate's parents in August 2013

> To mark my birth, the London Eye was lit up red, white and blue and the BT Tower and Trafalgar Square were also illuminated.

The day after my birth, both sets of grandparents, known widely as Prince Charles and Camilla plus Carole and Michael Middleton, visited me for the first time.

They all emerged from the hospital with huge smiles on their faces – but that was nothing compared to the grins shared by my parents William and Kate when they too showed up on the steps of the Lindo Wing to show me off to the world..

"It's very emotional," Mum told reporters. "It's such a special time. I think any parent will know what this feels like."

My dad was in a playful mood with the media and joked that he was glad his son, who weighed 8lb 6oz at birth, had his mother's looks.

"He's got a good pair of lungs on him, that's for sure," he added. "He's a big boy, he's quite heavy."

And with that, I was placed in my car seat and driven away from hospital and into my new life.

It was two days later that my name was announced by Kensington Palace. George Alexander Louis were the names chosen meaning I would also be referred to as His Royal Highness Prince George of Cambridge.

My new life had well and truly begun.

Above: A fan of the royal family camps out to wait for the new arrival

Right: A careful handover as son is passed from mother to father

When I was christened...

Very few events in the lives of the Royal Family are quiet, intimate affairs. However, my christening was exactly that.

Only 22 guests attended the service in the Chapel Royal at St James's Palace in London. It was an occasion for senior royals only, as well as four members of my mummy's family.

The Archbishop of Canterbury conducted the service, watched by my godparents; Oliver Baker, Emilia Jardine-Paterson, Earl Grosvenor, Jamie Lowther-Pinkerton, Julia Samuel, William van Cutsem and Zara Tindall.

Zara Tindall is, of course, my daddy's cousin, while the other godparents are all friends of William and Kate.

It was particularly poignant to see Julia Samuel as a godparent as she was very close to my late grandmother Diana, Princess of Wales, while Jamie Lowther-Pinkerton is a former aide to my daddy and has helped to prepare him for when he becomes King.

For the 45-minute ceremony my parents chose two hymns, two lessons and two anthems for the christening.

The hymns were Breathe on Me, Breath of God and Be Thou My Vision.

Lessons from St Luke and St John were read by Auntie Pippa and Uncle Harry, and the anthems were Blessed Jesus! Here We Stand and Lord Bless You and Keep You.

The anthems were sung by the Choir of Her Majesty's Chapel Royal, which performed at Mummy and Daddy's wedding, and once the ceremony was finished, I left the Chapel Royal in the arms of Mummy as we headed off for tea at Clarence House.

My outfit for his christening caused quite a stir – and rightly so!

On just my second public appearance – the first being on the steps of the Lindo Wing the day after my birth – I wore a replica of the original Royal Christening Gown.

The original version was designed in 1841 for Queen Victoria's eldest daughter, Victoria, the Princess Royal.

In the years since then, over 60 royals were christened in the gown but its age and increasing fragility meant it can no longer be worn.

However, all was not lost as my great grandmother the Queen asked her couturier, Angela Kelly, to craft a hand-made replica version in 2008.

I may have stolen the show in the gown but I was not the first to wear the replica garment.

That accolade goes to James, Viscount Severn, who wore it at his christening at Windsor Castle in April, 2008.

Selected guests arrive for Prince George's christening

William, Kate, George and the Archbishop of Canterbury

Royal enthusiasts gather outside St James' Palace

A huge christening card signed by 5000 people

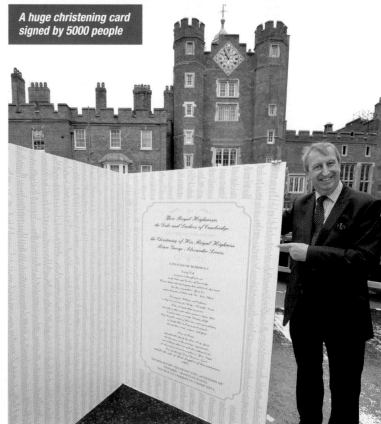

'Only 22 guests attended the service. It was an occasion for senior royals only as well as four members of the Middleton family'

Kate beams with pride as she holds George after the christening ceremony, which was attended by Prince Harry (left)

KEEPING A SPECIAL OCCASION ALIVE

One thing can be guaranteed whenever there is a royal birth, christening, wedding or funeral. Memorabilia will be churned out left, right and centre.

A quick peek online will show the weird and wonderful trinkets available to those wanting to remember a royal event.

For George's birth and christening, mugs, tea towels, DVDs, a tableware set and a commemorative medal were all available and around the country, souvenir shops noted record sales of keyrings, Prince George-embossed souvenir plates and a whole host of other memorabilia.

A Gold Proof Kilo Coin (left) and Silver Proof Kilo Coin (right) were struck to celebrate Prince George's christening

Queen Elizabeth II was christened in Buckingham Palace's private chapel

BREAKING THE MOULD

George was the first future monarch in recent times to be christened away from Buckingham Palace

The chance to catch up with friends, family and loved ones and celebrate a great day. Who doesn't love a good christening?

The royal family are no different.

Christenings are an important spiritual and social occasion for the royal family, especially as Prince George will one day carry the title 'Defender of the Faith and Supreme Governor of the Church of England'.

George was the first future monarch in modern times not to be baptised at Buckingham Palace with both his dad, William, and grandfather, Charles, christened in the palace's Music Room.

The Queen, who was not expected to be Queen when born, was christened in the Palace's private chapel in 1926.

Edward VIII, who later abdicated, was baptised at White Lodge in Richmond Park in 1894 and his brother George VI, who was not expected to be King, was christened at the Church of St Mary Magdalene close to the Sandringham estate in 1895.

William was baptised on August 4, 1982, at the age of six weeks, while the Prince of Wales was one month and one day old at his own christening.

The Queen was just over five weeks old when she was christened.

Princess Eugenie, Prince Andrew and the Duchess of York's daughter, was the first royal baby to have a public christening as she was baptised during morning service at the church of St Mary Magdalene at Sandringham just before Christmas in 1990.

Most royal christenings have gone to plan – but they've not always been plain sailing.

At Queen Victoria's in 1819, there was a dispute over what she should be called.

Her mother, the Duchess of Kent, had wanted to call her Georgiana Charlotte Augusta Alexandrina Victoria, but was overruled by a cantankerous Prince Regent, the future George IV, who dictated during the ceremony that she be called Alexandrina Victoria instead in tribute to the Russian Tsar Alexander I.

The Duchess was left distraught and broke down sobbing during the proceedings.

However, there were no such problems at George's christening as he left the church alongside his delighted parents.

Babes in arms

Top: **Prince Charles and Prince William were christened in Buckingham Palace's Music Room**

Middle left: **Princess Eugenie was the first royal baby to have a public christening**

Middle right: **Princess Anne with son Peter**

Left: **William steals the show at brother Harry's christening photo**

William, Kate
and
PARENTHOOD

KATE CAREFUL TO GIVE HER CHILDREN A 'NORMAL' UPBRINGING

Kate and William look at home in their new roles as parents

As with every mother across the globe, Kate Middleton's first days, weeks and months with her firstborn baby made for special moments.

However, most of those took place well and truly behind closed doors.

Following Prince George's much-snapped exit from the Lindo Wing, the young prince was rarely seen in public as William and Kate took time out to get to know their new son.

Throughout her pregnancy and following the birth, Kate has made it crystal clear that she wanted to be as 'normal' as possible and see George as often as other mothers see their children.

Being a child born into the royal family usually means a coterie of nurses and nannies bring you up but Kate never wanted that – and it showed.

Kate and William had been expected to attend the society wedding of James Meade and Lady Laura Marsham, daughter of the Earl of Romney, just six weeks after George's birth but in the end William attended on his own, with rumours circulating that Kate preferred to stay at home and out of the limelight as she cared for her six-week-old son.

Generally speaking, Kate's first 12 months following the birth of George were relatively low key. Apart from the three-week tour of Australia and New Zealand, both Kate and George remained practically unseen.

Before the birth of Prince George, Kate's last public ➤

Kate continued with her public appearances, but kept them to a minimum shortly after becoming a mum

Kate and George arrive in Wellington, New Zealand, on one of the prince's few public outings

'With George seeming to grow up in a happy and loving environment there's every reason to suppose the template has been set for how things are likely to go with the upbringing of the new arrival'

engagement was attending a ship naming ceremony at Ocean Terminal, Southampton, on June 13, 2013, and she remained out of the public eye until she joined William at the Ring O' Fire Anglesey Coastal Ultra Marathon a few months later in August.

After that, public appearances continued to be strictly rationed.

Kate joined William at the inaugural Tusk Conservation Awards at The Royal Society, London, in September before just a handful of other public appearances in 2013.

2014 followed the same pattern with Kate attending events at Northolt High School, Ealing, and the National Portrait Gallery in February, while the early part of the summer was taken up with a June event at the National Maritime Musuem in Greenwich as well as the Tour De France Grand Depart in Yorkshire on July 5.

However, apart from those events, Kate and George remained under the radar in that first year of the infant's life and that is further proof that the modern day royal family – unlike in earlier times – are doing all they can to ensure that Prince George can have a normal, happy and healthy childhood.

The fact that Kate and George were out of the public eye is also down to the stresses and strains of moving house as in the autumn of 2013, Prince William and his family moved into a 21-room apartment inside Kensington Palace.

'With George seeming to grow up in a happy and loving environment there's every reason to suppose the template has been set for how things are likely to go with the upbringing of Princess Charlotte.

HAPPY PARENTS CALL IN THE BABYSITTERS

Kate's first public appearance after the birth of Prince George came at the Holyhead Breakwater Country Park as she joined Prince William in starting the Ring O' Fire Anglesey Coastal Ultra Marathon.

The event is a gruelling 135-mile run that circumnavigates the whole of the island of Anglesey.

Kate mingled happily with the runners and those watching the tiring event and she told the waiting crowd that her own mother, Carole, was on babysitting duties.

"George is doing very well. He's with his granny at the moment. He's sleeping well but I know these things suddenly change," she said.

Kate and William looked very relaxed at the event and could feel at home in the area as they lived in a rented farmhouse in North Wales.

They have since moved to Kensington Palace but retain close links with Anglesey and North Wales in general.

Kate and William at the Holyhead Breakwater Country Park in North Wales in August 2013

BACK TO WORK FOR A 21ST CENTURY DAD

As is the case in many families, while mum Kate stayed out of the limelight with Prince George when he was a baby, dad Prince William returned to his job and his duties relatively quickly and royal engagements and appointments ensured the public saw plenty of the new father.

In 2013, William conducted 18 public engagements following the birth of George and his duties ranged from handing out Operational Service Medals, for deployment in Afghanistan, to soldiers of No. 2 Company, 1st Battalion Irish Guards, to attending the UK premiere of *Mandela: Long Walk to Freedom*, at the Odeon Leicester Square, London.

The start of 2014 was equally hectic, especially as it was announced that William would also be attending Cambridge University for a 10-week course in agricultural management, a move designed to help him take a hands-on role when he inherits the Duchy of Cornwall estate from his father.

Since then, William and Kate, known as the Earl and Countess of Strathearn in Scotland, have toured Perth and Kinross as well as embarking on their three-week tour of Australia and New Zealand together – although the star of the show Down Under was Prince George, rather than his royal parents.

William, as second in line to the throne, automatically has more duties and engagements than his wife but he has often demonstrated and spoken of his desire and willingness to help raise Prince George and his new sibling as much as possible. He may be a very busy man but he is also the epitome of a 21st century dad. He wants to be there and he wants to help.

And although he may have to clock up the air miles as part of his royal role, William looks certain to play a huge and defining role in his children's lives – just as Prince Charles has done with William and Harry.

William meets children at the Whenuapai Air Base in Auckland, New Zealand

'Although he may have to clock up the air miles as part of his royal role, William looks certain to play a huge and defining role in his children's lives'

William went back to school to study agricultural management at Cambridge University

Joining in story time with children at a new library in Birmingham

One will inherit the throne, the other is 'spare to the heir' but William and Harry are clearly close

THE SECOND CHILD

Harry a close example of how to be a 'spare to the heir'

Bringing a second child into the world is a wonderful blessing and a joyous occasion. It can also be a right royal pain...especially when you have the complication of being a member of one of the world's most celebrated families.

For William and Kate having a second child will bring many great times and add an extra dimension to what already seems like a dream family set-up, but the arrival of a sibling for George means they will face the challenges that having a second child will bring.

In terms of succession to the throne the Duke and Duchess of Cambridge have provided what has a little cruelly been dubbed a 'spare to the heir' and that means the second child will not only have the normal problem of fighting for an identity of its own as three becomes four, but the baby will also immediately be further down the pecking order in terms of the line of succession.

A psychologist who studied birth order since the 1960s – Dr Kevin Leman – said of the differences between a couple's first two children: "The one thing you can bet your paycheck

on is the firstborn and second-born in any given family are going to be different."

But will being second-born in royal circles give the new baby a disadvantage in life or is it a role you can make a success of?

The best place for the new baby to look is towards the previous 'spare to the heir' Uncle Harry.

The new baby's birth has pushed Harry further down the line of succession but William's younger brother has always known it was unlikely he would become king one day.

Prince Henry Charles Albert David of Wales (popularly known as Prince Harry) was born on September 15, 1984, at St. Mary's Hospital in London, just over two years after William's birth.

As a youngster Harry was described as quiet and reserved as compared to his then-rumbustious, outgoing older brother William. However, as each matured the character roles reversed, with William becoming the more shy and reflective of the two while Harry grew up to be friendly and charismatic.

With a low chance of ascension, the 'spare to the heir' has long tended to be the wilder child of a royal family.

Prince Andrew was often criticised for leading a wild-spending life, not to mention his marrying a woman who many have argued never quite fit the royal mould: Sarah Ferguson.

Prince Harry is certainly a popular royal and many see him as a link between the traditional royal family and the common folk but there's no doubt he has made a few high profile misjudgements in his private life having hit the headlines following scuffles with paparazzi, for enjoying the party life a little too much and even dressing as a Nazi soldier.

But there can be little doubt that there is much to admire about a man who does lots of work for charity and who was instrumental in setting up the Invictus Games for injured military personnel.

Whatever he does though, Harry is always likely to be seen as the less glamorous brother and he has spent his whole life being compared to William.

While they have always seemed to have a close relationship, William was the more accomplished student at school, going on to achieve three A-levels and a 2.1 degree in geography while Harry managed two lower grade A-levels.

Harry did, though, carve out a military career for himself culminating in him becoming an Apache helicopter pilot who served his country by being stationed in Afghanistan, although his 10-year career in the armed forces is due to end in the coming months.

Prince Andrew

What he will do next is not yet known but Harry has an important role to play in the evolution of the royal family.

He may never be king but in an age where questions are asked about the relevance of the monarchy in the modern world, Harry is one of the royals who has the ability to bridge the gap between the privilege of the royal family and the everyday people around them.

In essence, that is what a 'spare to the heir' must do; carve out a niche for themselves to give their lives purpose and help the royal family in any way they can.

If Prince Harry can help William and Kate's new arrival to find a place in the world, he will have done an excellent job as an uncle.

Uncle Harry will have a role to play in guiding brother William's latest arrival

Grandad Michael

Great Granny & Great Grandfather

Step-Granny Camilla

Uncle James

Granny Carole

Grandad Charles

Uncle Harry

Meet THE FAMILY

The latest royal arrival will receive plenty of love, care and attention from the Windsors and Middletons

THE arrival of baby George two years ago signalled a big change for the royal family but Kate and William will hope the birth of their second child will go just as smoothly.

Whether you are born into a life of privilege or you're a single mum living in the inner city, the love and support of your family after a child is born is vital – particularly in those first few challenging months.

And it seems that Kate and William have been blessed with a family network that is keen to help out wherever they can to be close to their youngest relatives.

Having been eager to spend as much time with George as possible there's no doubt that Prince Charles will want to play an equally important role as grandfather to the new arrival.

When news of Kate's second pregnancy was announced last year it was clear that Charles was very pleased with ➤

Auntie Pippa

FAMILY TREE

Prince George
22 July 2013

Princess Charlotte
2 May 2015

Catherine Middleton
09 January 1982

Prince William
21 June 1982

Pippa Middleton
1983

James Middleton
1987

Prince Harry
1984

Michael Middleton
1949

Carole Goldsmith
1955

Anne
1950

Andrew
1960

Edward
1964

Prince Charles
1948

Diana Spencer
1961 – died 1997

Camilla
1947

Peter Middleton
1920 – died 2010

Valerie Glassborrow
1924 – died 2006

Queen Elizabeth II
1926

Prince Phillip
1921

Richard Middleton
1878 – died 1951

Olive Lupton
1881 – died 1936

Edward VIII
1894 – died 1972
*(Abdicated the throne in 1936
to marry Wallis Simpson)*

George VI
1895 – died 1952

Lady Elizabeth Bowes-Lyon
1900 – died 2002

John Middleton
1839 – died 1887

Mary Asquith
1839 – died 1889

George V
1865 – died 1936

Princess Mary of Teck
1867 – died 1953

William Middleton
1807 – died 1884

Mary Ward
1811 – died 1859

King Edward VII
1841 – died 1910

Princess Alexandra
1844 – died 1925

Great Uncle Andrew

Great Uncle Edward

Great Auntie Anne

the news – even if he did display a level of partiality with regard to the gender of the baby.

"It's wonderful. I'm happy I'm going to be a grandfather again," he said last September.

"I'm looking forward to it – but I hope it will be a girl this time."

Before George was born it was thought that Charles might be a little intolerant of 'little people', as he calls them, as it was thought he didn't welcome having children running around his Highgrove residence.

But when he found out he was becoming a grandparent for the first time at the age of 64 he said: "I'm thrilled, marvellous. It's a lovely thought and I look forward enormously to that relationship. It's a very nice thought to become a grandfather in my old age, if I can say so."

This time around the pregnancy was announced via a statement from Clarence House.

If anyone was in any doubt about what the Queen and Prince Philip thought of the future arrival of another grandchild, the words of that statement said it all.

"Their Royal Highnesses The Duke and Duchess of Cambridge are very pleased to announce that The Duchess of Cambridge is expecting their second child.

"The Queen and members of both families are delighted with the news."

Princes Andrew and Edward, and Anne, the Princess Royal, are likely to have more of a background role, but can certainly offer plenty of advice given they are all parents to two children.

Prince Harry, meanwhile, has probably been the most vocal in his reaction to news he will become an uncle for the second time.

Famous for not taking life too seriously Harry told the media: "I can't wait to see my brother suffer more."

And his thoughts on seeing his brother looking after a baby girl? "[I would] love to see him try and cope with that."

On a serious note he did say that he hoped the pregnancy, birth and immediate aftermath passed by successfully for his brother and sister-in-law.

"I hope the two of them have the opportunity to go through the process again with a little bit of peace and quiet," Harry explained.

He even shared that he thinks little Prince George will be "over-the-moon" once he has a little brother or sister to play with.

The birth of George did give Harry a chance to reflect on his role as an uncle – a role he will no doubt now carry out doubly-well.

When asked about his mission as an uncle to George, Harry simply said it's "to make sure he has a good upbringing, and keep him out of harm's way and to make sure he has fun. The rest I'll leave to the parents."

As for the Middletons, Kate is very close to her sister Pippa, who will no doubt be around to lend a hand whenever called upon, while a mother's own parents – in this case Carole and Michael Middleton – are usually relied upon to lend lots of support. That is the perfect scenario for William and Kate who want to keep care of their children in the family as much as possible.

Given that William is known to admire the closeness of the Middletons, he will feel more relaxed about his wife and children having such loving assistance whenever he is away.

NEXT IN *Line*

Baby fourth in line behind brother, father and patient grandfather

THE birth of Wiliam and Kate's baby means their offspring now occupy the number three and four slots in the line of succession to the throne.

As a sibling to Prince George, the Duke and Duchess of Cambridge's second child will not be expected to be crowned sovereign.

But second-born royal children – often dubbed the "spare to heir" – have on occasion ended up as monarch.

The country's last king, George VI, was not meant to accede to the throne and only did so when his older brother Edward VIII abdicated over his love for American divorcee Wallis Simpson in 1936.

George VI's father, George V, was also not destined to wear the crown. But he outlived his older brother the Duke of Clarence and Avondale – Prince Albert Victor – who died from flu in 1892. George V became King in 1910.

William and Kate's new baby will be a great-grandchild to the Queen and a great-great-great-great-great-grandchild of Queen Victoria.

The new baby's arrival means Prince Harry will shift down the line of succession to fifth, while the Duke of York will move to sixth place and princesses Beatrice and Eugenie to seventh and eighth.

The baby will be a prince or princess thanks to the Queen, who stepped in ahead of Prince George's birth to ensure all William's children would become HRHs with fitting titles.

The Queen issued a Letters Patent under the Great Seal

16

2

3

Queen Victoria (top), the longest-reigning monarch at the time of the new baby's birth, and Edward VII, who waited nearly 60 years to succeed her

of the Realm in December 2012 when Kate was just a few months pregnant, declaring "all the children of the eldest son of the Prince of Wales should have and enjoy the style, title and attribute of royal highness with the titular dignity of prince or princess prefixed to their Christian names or with such other titles of honour".

All being well Prince George is unlikely to take the crown for a long time but he probably won't have to be as patient as the Prince of Wales.

Charles has waited longer than anyone else in history to ascend to the throne, having been next in line since King George VI's death in 1952 when he was just three years old.

The previous record holder was Edward VII who succeeded Queen Victoria in 1901 after a wait of 59 years, two months and 13 days. Charles passed that mark in April 2011.

So far the Queen has resisted any suggestion that she abdicate to allow her eldest son to take over.

There has been a recent precedent in the Netherlands where 75-year-old Queen Beatrix abdicated and son Prince Willem-Alexander became King.

Although they won't directly affect Charles and William's eventual succession, changes are afoot to the royal line as the Succession To The Crown Act was passed by parliament in April 2013.

The main consequence of the Act, which for many was long overdue, is to end the principle of sons taking precedence over daughters as heirs to the throne. It also lifts the bar on the sovereign and prospective heirs from marrying a Catholic.

The line of succession

SOVEREIGN

1. The Prince of Wales
2. The Duke of Cambridge
3. Prince George of Cambridge
4. Princess Charlotte of Cambridge
5. Prince Henry of Wales
6. The Duke of York
7. Princess Beatrice of York
8. Princess Eugenie of York
9. The Earl of Wessex
10. Viscount Severn
11. The Lady Louise Mountbatten-Windsor
12. The Princess Royal
13. Mr. Peter Phillips
14. Miss Savannah Phillips
15. Miss Isla Phillips
16. Mrs. Michael Tindall
17. Miss Mia Tindall
18. Viscount Linley
19. The Hon. Charles Armstrong-Jones
20. The Hon. Margarita Armstrong-Jones
21. The Lady Sarah Chatto
22. Mr. Samuel Chatto
23. Mr. Arthur Chatto
24. The Duke of Gloucester
25. Earl of Ulster
26. Lord Culloden
27. The Lady Cosima Windsor
28. The Lady Davina Lewis
29. Master Tane Lewis
30. Miss Senna Lewis
31. The Lady Rose Gilman
32. Master Rufus Gilman
33. Miss Lyla Gilman
34. The Duke of Kent
35. The Lady Amelia Windsor
36. The Lady Helen Taylor
37. Mr. Columbus Taylor
38. Mr. Cassius Taylor
39. Miss Eloise Taylor
40. Miss Estella Taylor

Taken from www.royal.gov.uk

Growing up
IN THE
SPOTLIGHT

Living life in the glare of the nation will be tough at times, but royal children don't have to look far for advice on how to cope with it...

They may not always like it but the unavoidable truth for the royal family is that they live their entire lives under the spotlight.

It cannot be easy to be constantly followed around by paparazzi and members of the press, keen for a quote and a headline and something exciting to fill the next day's papers.

However, it comes with the territory and most of the time the royal family cope brilliantly with the interest in their lives.

Growing up is tough at the best of times and that is only exacerbated by the glare of the spotlight and William and Kate's second child is likely to feel that as much as Prince George and the other high profile royals.

Yet one bonus for George and his sibling is that they only have to look around them for hints, tips and advice for how to cope with the public's interest.

Every single member of their family, from their great-grandmother to their Uncle Harry, have learned how to cope with the situation.

The Queen's upbringing was actually very quiet because she was never expected to become the monarch.

It was only when her uncle, King Edward VIII, abdicated in 1938, that she moved up to heir to the throne as her father, King George VI, took over.

Until then, she had lived a relatively normal life alongside her sister Margaret.

However, her own children did not really enjoy the same privilege. Following his birth in 1948, interest in Prince Charles was immediate and overwhelming as newspapers wanted to know all about his life.

As he grew up, Charles found himself at the centre of plenty of public scrutiny, particularly when he attended Gordonstoun school in Scotland. Prince Charles hated the place and that made growing up there doubly hard.

His three siblings, Princess Anne, Prince Andrew and Prince Edward also had their fair share of ups and downs as they grew up, especially Prince Edward, who dropped out of Royal Marine training in 1987, much to the public's derision.

Daddy's life through a lens

Prince William's childhood was recorded at every stage whether he was...

cuddling Mummy...

dribbling...

flying...

being cheeky...

sheltering...

starting school...

looking sheepish...

pushing little brother around...

enjoying Christmas...

watching tennis...

relaxing with Dad...

or grieving...

Charles'
2nd birthday

Charles'
3rd birthday

Charles'
4th birthday

George's grandfather Prince Charles has also lived a life under the microscope as these pictures taken on his birthdays illustrate

> All the main events in a royal's life are documented by the media and by the public so christenings, first days at school, sporting achievements and any ups and downs are all events the outside world will take an interest in.

Prince William had to grimace his way through his opening day at Eton College in 1995 and it was the same when he went to the University of St. Andrew's in 2001.

He had also had his fair share of bumps and bruises by that point, especially back in 1991 when he was accidently whacked with a golf club. He had to undergo surgery for a depressed skull fracture at Great Ormond Street Hospital which has left him, in his own words, with a "Harry Potter-style" scar.

William's younger brother, Harry, is another who has spent his life under the glare but it is something he is now used to and he will pass his own perspective on in his role as an uncle.

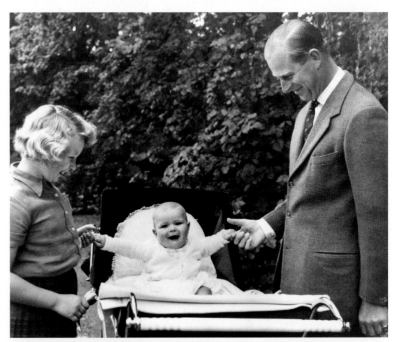

Prince Harry (right), aged four, dressed as a shepherd ahead of a nursery nativity play

Charles' 5th birthday

Charles' 6th birthday

Charles' 7th birthday

'Christenings, first days at school, sporting achievements and any ups and downs are all events the outside world will take an interest in'

Growing up in public

Far left above: **Prince Andrew with sister Anne and the Duke of Edinburgh in 1960**

Far left below: **Prince Charles with William and Harry at Klosters in 2000**

Left: **The Queen and Duke of Edinburgh – and a pet corgi – with all their children in Windsor**

Above: **A newspaper page from 1991 is an example of the interest shown in the royal family**

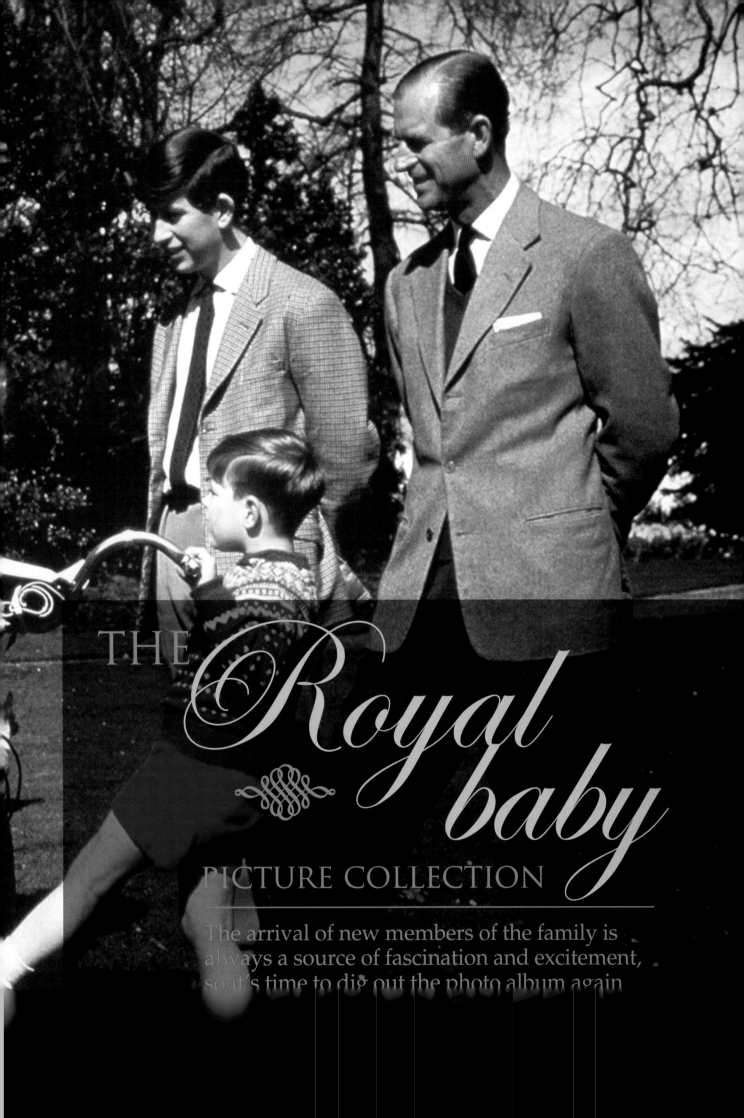

THE Royal baby

PICTURE COLLECTION

The arrival of new members of the family is always a source of fascination and excitement, so it's time to dig out the photo album again

The future King Edward VIII and King George VI in their prams, 1895

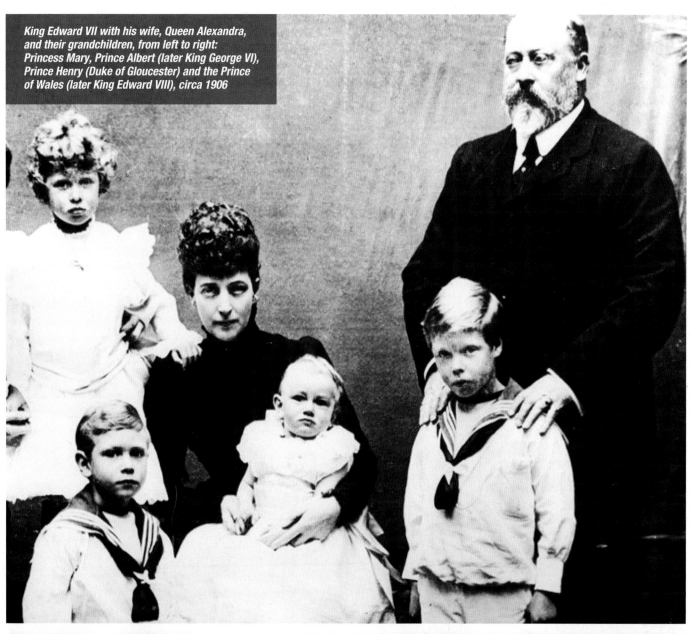

King Edward VII with his wife, Queen Alexandra, and their grandchildren, from left to right: Princess Mary, Prince Albert (later King George VI), Prince Henry (Duke of Gloucester) and the Prince of Wales (later King Edward VIII), circa 1906

The future Queen Mother in 1902 with an elder sister

King George V and Queen Alexandra pose with their daughter, Princess Mary, and baby, July 1923

ELIZABETH, 21.04.1926

The woman who, at the time of writing, is closing in on being the longest reigning monarch in British history was born at 2.40am at No. 17 Bruton Street, Mayfair, the London town house of the Earl and Countess of Strathmore, the parents of the then Duchess of York (later to become the beloved Queen Mother).

At 10am a statement confirmed that both mother and daughter were making "satisfactory progress" following the birth. It also said that "a certain line of treatment was successfully adopted", which was a cryptic method for avoiding saying that Elizabeth had been delivered by Caesarean section.

Curiously, the following day's Daily Mirror reported that 'in accordance with custom the Home Secretary (Sir William Joynson-Hicks) was summoned to be at hand at the birth'.

It was a time of turmoil in Britain with Joynson-Hicks dragged away from talks to try and resolve a coal dispute, which would culminate in the commencement of the General Strike in May when for six days industries and services ground to a halt and workers took to the streets.

The royal birth was a source of joy and escapism for the public, as well as the immediate family. People lined the street outside Bruton Street, waiting to glimpse visitors. King George V and Queen Mary travelled by car from Windsor to see their daughter-in-law. The Prince of Wales, the Duke of York's older brother, telegraphed congratulations from Biarritz.

Exactly a month after the birth, the first picture of the new princess was released and her name was revealed: Elizabeth Alexandra Mary. Elizabeth after her mother, Alexandra after the late Queen Mother and Mary after the then Queen.

The Daily Mirror of April 22 had suggested she may be named Elizabeth. She was christened on May 29 in the private chapel at Buckingham Palace. Water brought from the River Jordan was used.

IN THE NEWS:
Prime Minister Stanley Baldwin was due to meet mineowners as the coal dispute continued

The then Duke and Duchess of York with the days-old Princess Elizabeth, April 1926

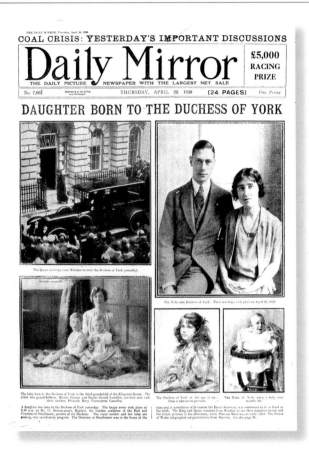

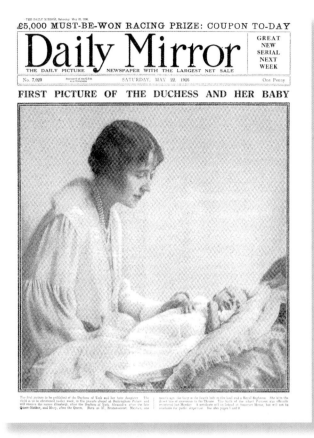

Daily Mirror front pages celebrating Elizabeth's arrival

A private photograph of baby Elizabeth and her parents, taken by a young holidaying couple whose car had broken down outside the royal couple's Scottish cottage and knocked on the door for help. The Duke and Duchess were happy to assist, providing water for the tourists to fill up their leaking radiator

Prince Philip, Elizabeth's future husband, aged 12 months in 1922

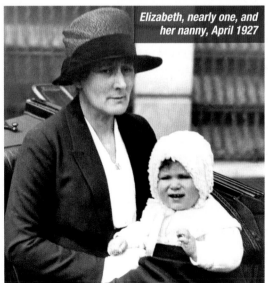

Elizabeth, nearly one, and her nanny, April 1927

CHARLES, 15.11.1948

The birth of Princess Elizabeth's first child was already well anticipated before his arrival on Sunday, November 14, 1948.

From early dawn on the 14th, hundreds of people gathered outside Buckingham Palace, watching and waiting.

Before going into labour, Elizabeth, described as 'radiant and cheerful' by the Daily Mirror, lunched with her husband, Prince Philip, and the King and Queen. Lobster, tongue and ham salad was on the menu.

When her son arrived at 9.14pm on the 14th, he weighed 7lb 6oz and was said to have fair hair like his father. He was delivered at Buckingham Palace.

At 9am on the 15th, the king's piper, Alec MacDonald, played a stirring Scottish tune on the bagpipes in the gardens of the Palace. Elizabeth smiled at the sound as, the Daily Mirror reported: 'It is her dearest wish that her son should share her love of Scotland and its traditions.'

The Mirror's celebratory editorial said: 'The aspect of the happy event which is likely to have struck people most forcibly is its highly modern character. This was shown in the ease and normality of the birth, and in the pre-natal behaviour of the mother. Clearly we have a royal family who have no sympathy with old-fashioned ideas in regard to the important matter of maternity.'

Like his mother, the baby boy's name was revealed a month after the birth on December 14, the eve of his christening. It was to be Charles Philip Arthur George, chosen for "personal and private reasons".

It was the first time in two centuries that Britain had a Prince Charles.

IN THE NEWS:

The British film industry was having to cut costs with film stars and producers asked to take a voluntary 25% cut in salaries

The Labour government said Britain was on the verge of a steel age, as it prepared to nationalise the industry

AT THE CINEMA:
Bonnie Prince Charlie (!)

A proud mum with her first child at his christening, Buckingham Palace, December 1948

A family portrait with King George VI on the left

Aged five months

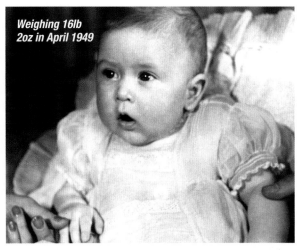

Weighing 16lb 2oz in April 1949

Lifted up by Dad in the grounds of Windlesham Moor, Surrey, July 1949

Playing in the cot outside on a summer's day

ANNE, 15.08.1950

Less than two years after the birth of Charles, Princess Elizabeth was delighted to have a daughter, who was safely delivered at Clarence House.

Weighing 6lb, a girl had been the preference for Elizabeth and Prince Philip, according to the Daily Mirror's report the following day.

A dispatch rider left Clarence House just after the birth and went straight to the Home Office with news of the birth. From there, the story was flashed all round the world.

Waiting crowds learned of the birth when a secretary, accompanied by Prince Philip's personal detective, placed a sheet of paper inside an oak-framed notice board, which read: '15th August 1950. HRH Princess Elizabeth was safely delivered of a Princess at 11.50am today. HRH and her daughter are both doing well.'

The crowds surged forward and when the news was digested, cheers sounded for the new princess.

The Daily Mirror's editorial read: 'Amid the stresses and anxieties that have come to make up the world's daily news, the people of Britain and the Commonwealth will be glad to turn their eyes to this family occasion for congratulation and rejoicing.'

The girl's name was revealed when she was two weeks old: Anne Elizabeth Alice Louise. It was reported that the first name had been chosen before the birth. For the previous three years, Anne/Ann had been the most popular girl's name, according to the announcements of births in The Times.

Obviously, Elizabeth was the Christian name of her mother and grandmother, Alice the name of Prince Philip's mother and Louise the feminine form of Louis – Earl (Louis) Mountbatten, then Chief of the Defence Staff – was Philip's uncle.

Anne made her first public appearance on the evening of September 17, heading for Balmoral with her mother on the 6.55 sleeper from King's Cross Station.

IN THE NEWS:
The Korean war raged between American and British troops and communist forces

AT THE CINEMA:
Sunset Boulevard

Above:
Anne's christening at Buckingham Palace, with Queen Mary pottering about in the background, October 1950

Right:
A portrait in the private sitting room of Clarence House, January 1951

Below:
The Daily Mirror carries the first picture of Princess Anne as she receives a kiss from her brother, September 1950

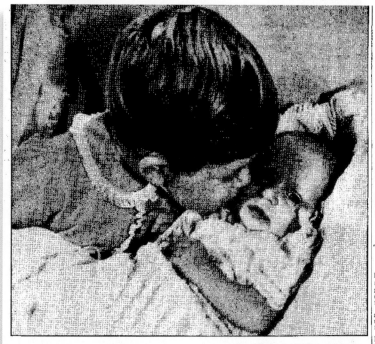

Princess Anne—the first picture

The first pictures of Princess Anne, daughter of Princess Elizabeth and the Duke of Edinburgh, are released this morning. They were taken by Cecil Beaton. Here are the little Princess and her brother Prince Charles, who will be two years old in November.
—Another picture, back page.

A proud grandmother on her 60th birthday, holding baby Andrew as Charles and Anne watch on

ANDREW, 19.02.1960

Princess Elizabeth had become Queen Elizabeth II by the time she gave birth to her third child, nearly 10 years after Anne.

Prompted by the frequent comings and goings of royal doctors, a crowd of nearly 1,000 people waited outside Buckingham Palace on the evening of February 18 1960, anticipating the new arrival. Shortly after 10pm two officials of the royal household emerged to shouts of "What is it – a boy or a girl?" However, there was a sense of anti-climax when they told those gathered that the birth was not imminent.

It was at 3.30pm the following day when a boy eventually arrived, the news confirmed to those outside 45 minutes later by Palace superintendent Stanley Williams who placed a bulletin on the Palace railings. A loud triumphant cry of "it's a boy" broke out. He weighed 7lb 3oz. Bells rang in celebration all over the country.

Appropriately, given the baby's future career, the Admiralty sent an order to all ships and naval bases: 'Splice the mainbrace'. This meant that rum would be issued to toast the birth.

A 4ft-high stork made of hundreds of white flowers arrived at the Palace in a Jaguar. There was no indication who sent the present.

His name, Andrew Albert Christian Edward, was revealed on March 22, together with the first pictures of the new prince.

Andrew and Albert were the names of his grandfathers; Christian came from his great-great-great grandfather – King Christian the IV of Denmark – and Edward from his great-great grandfather – King Edward VII.

Christened on April 8, he was the first Prince Andrew for 500 years.

IN THE NEWS:
It was revealed that Prime Minister Harold Macmillan would decide whether to allow House of Commons debates to be televised

ON THE BOX:
Emergency Ward 10
Take Your Pick

TOP OF THE CHARTS:
Why, Anthony Newley

EDWARD, 10.03.1964

The Queen's fourth and final child was a son who arrived a week early. He came into the world at 8.20pm on Tuesday, March 10 at Buckingham Palace, weighing 5lb 7oz.

Immediately after the birth Prince Philip telephoned the news to the Queen Mother at Clarence House, Princess Margaret at Kensington Palace, Prince Charles at Gordonstoun School and Princess Anne at Benenden School.

The Queen gave birth in the Belgian Suite at the Palace. Her five-man medical team was headed by Sir John Peel, the gynaecologist who was present at the births of all her children.

ITV interrupted the opening of The Plane Makers at 9.13pm to announce the birth in a news flash. The BBC waited another two minutes for a scheduled bulletin.

Royal Navy ships fired their guns in salute and 12 RAF Lightnings flew over London, while flowers arrived at the Palace 'in a non-stop stream'.

Prince Andrew, then four, wanted to give his little brother a well-worn teddy bear but when he was told it was too big, he took it to bed himself.

It was six weeks after the birth before the baby's name was revealed – Edward Antony Richard Louis.

Edward and Richard were former kings; Louis was in honour of Earl (Louis) Mountbatten – Prince Philip's favourite uncle, while Antony, which had never been used before in the royal family, was a compliment to Princess Margaret's then husband, Antony Armstrong-Jones.

Edward was christened on June 12, when he was 14 weeks old.

IN THE NEWS:
Britain's 7,000-strong peace force was struggling to maintain order in Cyprus as fighting escalated between Greek and Turkish Cypriots

Jack Ruby was being tried for the murder of Lee Harvey Oswald

ON THE BOX:
Big Night Out with Mike and Bernie Winters

TOP OF THE CHARTS:
Anyone Who Had A Heart, Cilla Black

A special guest at Trooping the Colour, June 1964

The Queen, Andrew and baby Edward in his crib, June 1964

A relaxed stroll in Windsor on the Queen's 39th birthday, April 1965

Andrew fetches a flower...

...which Anne lifts above Edward's head

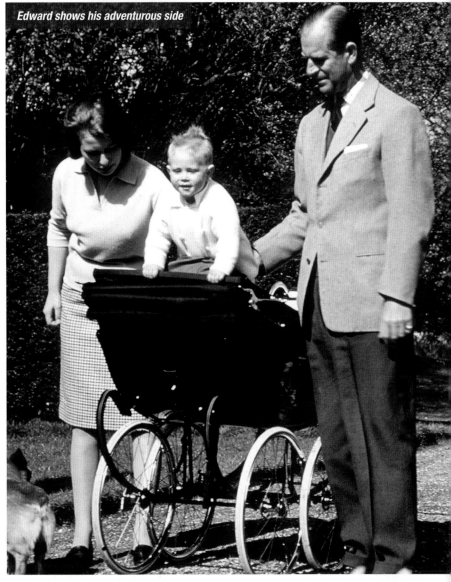

Edward shows his adventurous side

WILLIAM, 21.06.1982

There was a special sense of excitement surrounding the arrival of William, given his status as heir to the throne.

Princess Diana, who was still driving her Ford Escort the day before the birth, believed she was going to give birth on her 21st birthday – July 1 – but in the event her first child came 10 days earlier.

He weighed 7lb 1½oz when born at 9.03pm on a rainy evening after a 16-hour labour. When the news was announced, cheers erupted among those waiting expectantly outside St Mary's Hospital in Paddington. Before long, Prince Charles emerged to greet those outside and share his joy with the crowd, who joyously chanted "it's a boy" and "we want more".

In Buckingham Palace, the Queen was delighted when she was told that the baby had been born safely. She visited her new grandchild the following morning. Prince Andrew heard about the birth while serving with the Falklands task force, while Princess Anne was visiting the USA.

Mother and child left hospital 21 hours after he was delivered. Prince William was officially named seven days later, his full title being William Arthur Philip Louis.

The last King William was William IV, who was succeeded by Queen Victoria in 1837. Arthur was one of Prince Charles's own names, Philip came from the Duke of Edinburgh while Louis was a nod to the much-missed Earl Mountbatten, killed by an IRA bomb three years earlier.

William was christened two months later as a new royal era began.

IN THE NEWS:
Celebrations continued after Britain liberated the Falkland Islands from the Argentinian Junta

England had qualified for the second stage of the World Cup in Spain after winning their opening matches against France and Czechoslovakia

ON THE BOX:
Triangle
Wogan

TOP OF THE CHARTS:
Goody Two Shoes, Adam Ant

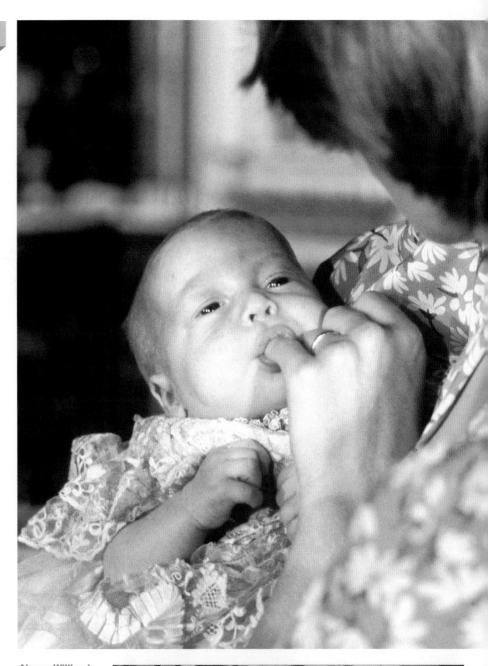

Above: William's christening at Buckingham Palace, August 1982

Right: Charles and Diana leave hospital clutching baby William in June 1982

Diana, Harry, William and Charles, 1985

DAILY **Mirror** **The best costs less** **16p**

1·59

day, September 17, 1984 FORWARD WITH BRITAIN ★ 16p

WILD ABOUT HARRY

PRINCESS
Diana presents her second son, Prince Harry, to the world. A world that is going wild about Harry, as he will be known.

Cradling him tenderly but firmly in her arms Diana left St. Mary's Hospital in Paddington, North London, yesterday after a stay of just 31 hours.

It was a day of smiles and joy. But in Diana's face there was something more. A mother's pride in her achievement.

Picture: BILL KENNEDY

● Royal Baby Special—see pages 2, 3, 16 and 17

MAXWELL GOES FOR BROACKES See Page 5.

Leaving hospital, September 1984

Diana and Harry, July 1985

HARRY, 15.09.1984

The second child of Prince Charles and Princess Diana broke with royal tradition in that he was named almost immediately.

Henry Charles Albert David – to be known as Prince Harry – was five days late when he eventually arrived at St Mary's Hospital, Paddington.

Of course, Henry has strong royal connotations, given it has been the name for eight kings. Charles came from Harry's father and Diana's brother. Albert, also common in the Spencer family, was the name of King George VI and Queen Victoria's husband, while David was the name of the Queen Mother's brother, David Bowes-Lyon.

Diana had been driven to hospital at 7.30am on September 15, with the birth finally happening at 4.20pm. It was a smooth and trouble-free labour.

The Queen was telephoned in Balmoral by Charles less than half an hour after Harry's arrival to be given the good news.

After one night at St Mary's, Diana, Harry and Charles left the hospital together at 2.30pm the following day.

After dropping them off at Kensington Palace, where Prince William was waiting, Charles picked up his polo gear and headed out to Windsor for a match, where he scored a hat-trick.

As for William, apparently his excited squeals woke up his baby brother.

Harry was christened at Windsor Castle on December 27.

IN THE NEWS:
The miner's strike was into its 27th week and a settlement seemed a long way off as peace talks between the National Coal Board and NUM collapsed

ON THE BOX:
The A-Team
The Paul Daniels Magic Show
Dynasty

TOP OF THE CHARTS:
I Just Called To Say I Love You, Stevie Wonder

15.11.1977

PETER PHILLIPS

In her silver jubilee year, the Queen became a grandmother when Princess Anne gave birth to a boy.

Wearing a broad grin, she told 800 guests "I'm sorry I'm late, but my daughter has given birth to a boy – and now I'm a grandmother" during an investiture ceremony at Buckingham Palace.

Captain Mark Phillips showed the royal family were adapting to changing times by being present at the birth.

Almost a month after coming into the world, the boy was named Peter Mark Andrew without a title, becoming the first royal baby to be born a commoner for 500 years. He was christened on December 22.

IN THE NEWS:
The Army's Green Goddesses were mobilised as Britain's firefighters went on strike

ON THE BOX:
It Ain't Half Hot Mum
Charlie's Angels

TOP OF THE CHARTS:
Name of the Game, Abba

The Queen, Anne and baby Peter at his christening, December 1977

Zara with big brother, November 1982

15.05.1981

ZARA PHILLIPS

Princess Anne's second child was a girl weighing 8lb 10oz, arriving just six hours after she was driven to St Mary's Hospital in Paddington by her private detective.

After the "perfectly normal" delivery, Anne was said to have joked: "Right, Mark and I have done our bit. Now it's up to Charles and Diana (who were due to marry two months later)."

It was almost four weeks before the girl was named – Zara Anne Elizabeth. A Buckingham Palace spokesman said: "Princess Anne and Captain Phillips just liked the name. They don't know anyone called Zara, and she is not named after anyone." Like her brother, Peter, Zara was not given a royal title.

IN THE NEWS:
The Pope was recovering from surgery after he was shot four times in Vatican City

ON THE BOX:
The Professionals
Knots Landing

TOP OF THE CHARTS:
Stand And Deliver, Adam Ant

08.11.2003

LOUISE

Lady Louise was born prematurely on November 8, 2003, at Frimley Park Hospital in Surrey after her mother was rushed there by ambulance from the Wessex home at Bagshot Park, Surrey.

Prince Edward was not present for the birth because it came so suddenly.

Her name was announced on November 27 and she was baptised in the Private Chapel of Windsor Castle on April 24, 2004.

08.08.88

BEATRICE

The Duke and Duchess of York celebrated their first child when a girl was born on the eighth day of the eighth month in 1988.

Prince Andrew drove his wife to London's Portland Hospital, arriving at 9.55am, and it was 8.18pm that evening when his daughter came into the world following an induced birth. There were no complications.

Mum and daughter left hospital four days after the birth – and immediately became the youngest royal to fly as she jetted to Scotland to spend time with the Queen at Balmoral.

She was named Beatrice Elizabeth Mary when two weeks old and christened shortly before Christmas.

IN THE NEWS:
A search for the body of Moors murder victim Keith Bennett was ongoing

ON THE BOX:
Ever Decreasing Circles
Rough Guide to Europe

TOP OF THE CHARTS:
The Only Way Is Up, Yazz and the Plastic Population

An official portrait at Balmoral when Beatrice was two weeks old

The royal family leave the church after Eugenie's christening

23.03.1990

EUGENIE

A little over 18 months after Beatrice's birth, the Duchess of York gave birth to another girl, with a Caesarean section required.

The girl, weighing 7lb 2oz, was born at 7.58pm, less than four hours after Fergie had arrived at hospital.

The baby left hospital a week after the birth, and on the same day was named Eugenie Victoria Helena.

Eugenie was a granddaughter of Queen Victoria. Victoria speaks for itself and Helena was the name of Queen Victoria's third daughter.

IN THE NEWS:
Labour won a landslide victory in the Mid-Staffordshire by-election, with the Tories losing thousands of votes

ON THE BOX:
A Bit of Fry and Laurie
Cheers
Surprise! Surprise!

TOP OF THE CHARTS:
Dub Be Good To Me, Beats International and Lindy Layton

17.12.2007

JAMES

Lord Severn was born by Caesarean section on December 17, 2007, at Frimley Park Hospital. Prince Edward, who was present for the birth of his second child, remarked that the birth was "a lot calmer than last time" (a reference to the emergency delivery of their first child, Lady Louise) and that his son was "like most babies, rather small, very cute and very cuddly."

Four days later his names were announced as James Alexander Philip Theo.

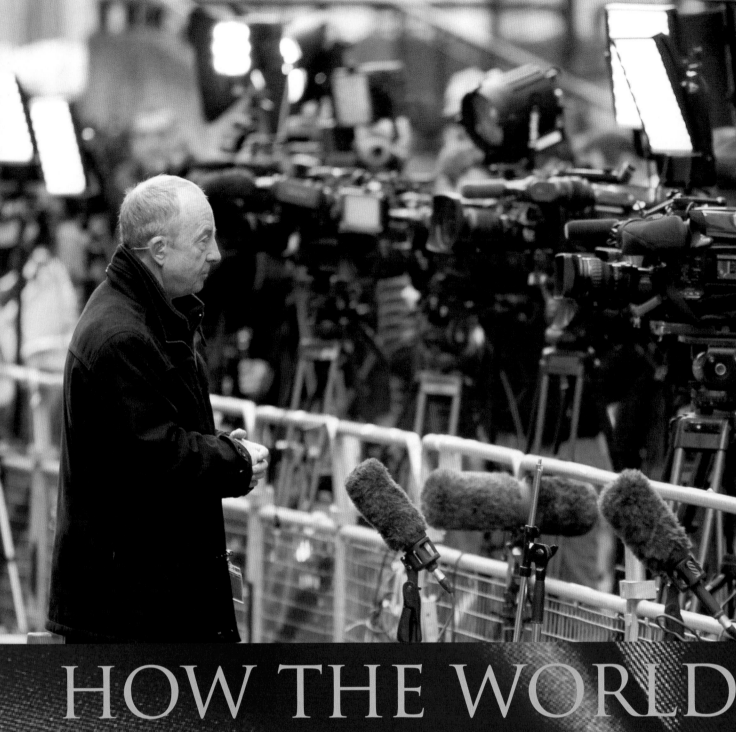

HOW THE WORLD

Once Charlotte's birth was announced, Twitter responded...

KENSINGTON PALACE:
Their Royal Highnesses would like to thank all staff at the hospital for the care and treatment they have all received.

LORD CHARLES SPENCER, PRINCESS DIANA'S BROTHER:
Perfect names. My 2-year-old Charlotte Diana will be thrilled at cousinly name-sharing.

ROSA MONCKTON, PRINCESS DIANA'S BEST FRIEND:
Diana's spirit lives on in her sons, and now her name lives on in her granddaughter. #CharlotteElizabethDiana

DISNEY:
Special delivery! #RoyalBaby

Diana's brother, Lord Charles Spencer, was delighted to hear the names chosen

REACTED...

and this is what people had to say

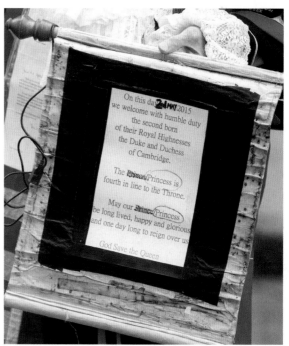

DAVID CAMERON:
Congratulations to the Duke and Duchess of Cambridge on the birth of their baby girl. I'm absolutely delighted for them.

HARRY POTTER AUTHOR JK ROWLING:
I was hoping for Nymphadora but no, not even a middle name.

AMERICAN TV HOST ELLEN DEGENERES:
The Princess is Charlotte Elizabeth Diana! A perfect name. I don't care that I ran out of room writing it on the Diaper Genie I got them.

APPRENTICE HIT LUISA ZISSMAN:
Princess Charlotte Elizabeth Diana! Yay we know the name. So happy Diana is in there, even if it does come after Elizabeth!

POP STAR CHERYL FERNDANDEZ-VERSINI:
Congratulations William and Kate. So excited to see our new little princess!! #itsagirl

TV PRESENTER CHARLIE WEBSTER:
Funny how many messages I keep getting about Princess Charlotte. Great name I have to say meaning 'strong and virile.' #PrincessCharlotte

MODEL CARA DELEVINGNE:
The new princess should be called Alice. If I am right, I win a pony.

GEORDIE SHORE'S CHARLOTTE CROSBY:
Well well well PRINCESS CHARLOTTE. What a bloody great name! Good choice Kate and Wills.
BIG UP YASELF (sic)

**WELCOME TO THE WORLD
HRH PRINCESS CHARLOTTE
OF CAMBRIDGE**